John Everett Millais

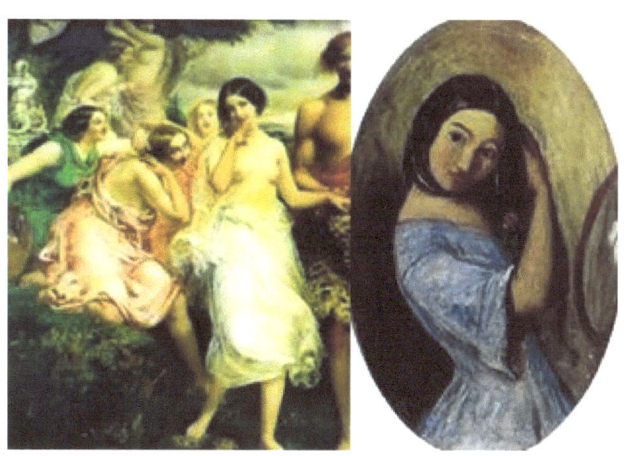

Edited by Lacey Belinda Smith

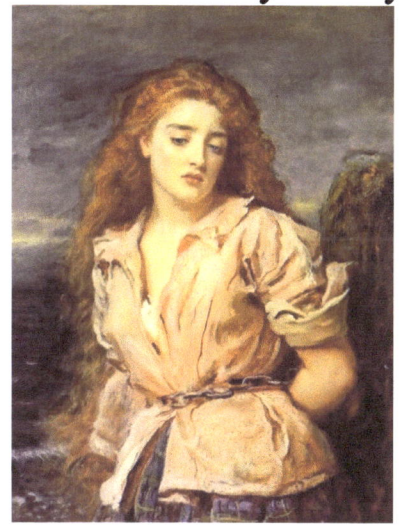

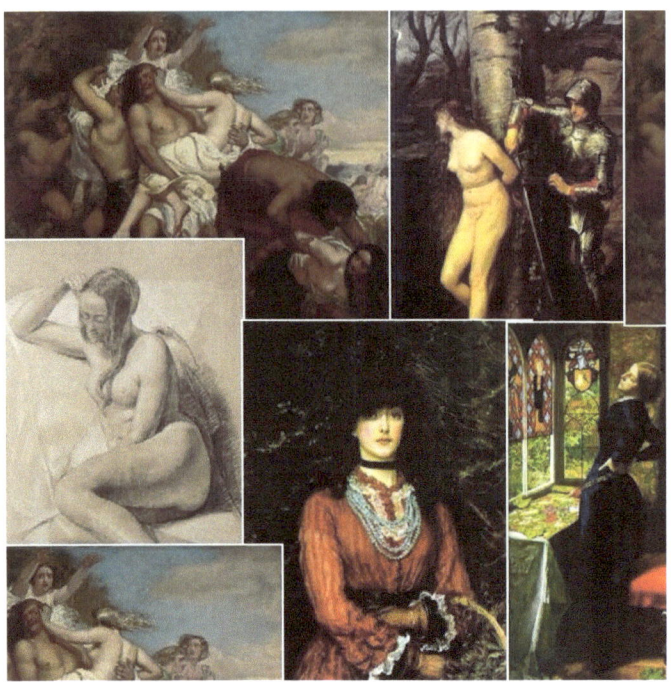

SIR JOHN EVERETT MILLAIS

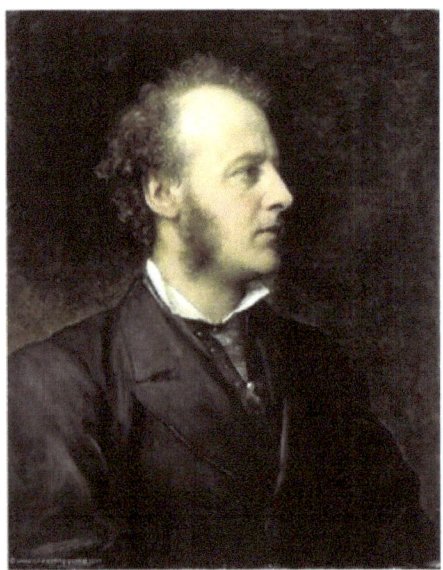

Portrait of Sir John Everett Millais by George Frederic Watts

British Artist--painting, printmaking, drawing--Pre-Raphaelite Brotherhood
1829; Southampton, United Kingdom-- 13 August 1896; London, United Kingdom

Romanticism, Realism movements

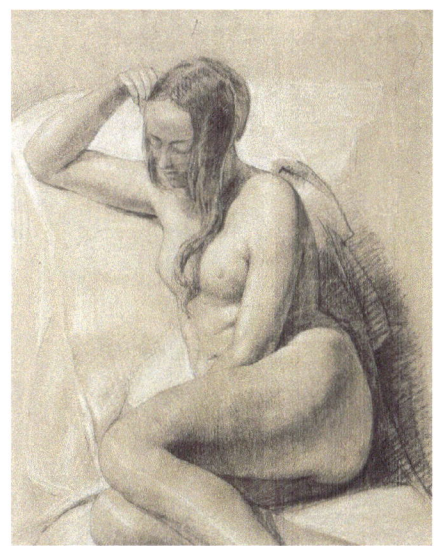

Reclining female nude (study)--*1845*

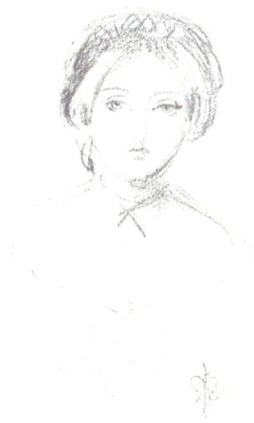

An English beauty (after John Leech)

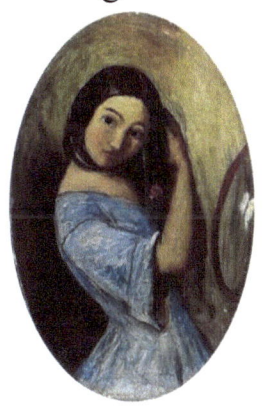

A Young Girl-Combing Her Hair--Romanticism

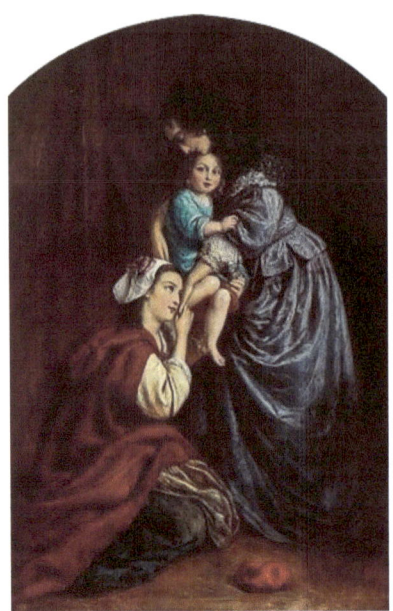

The exiles

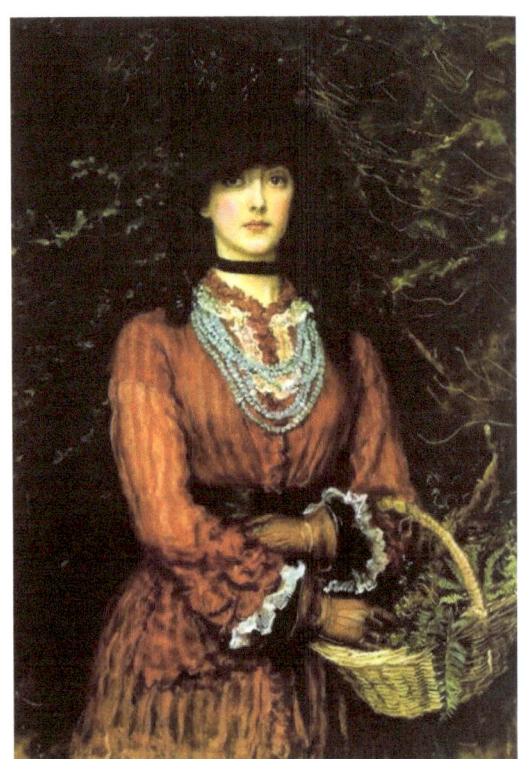

Miss Eveleen Tennant--Realism

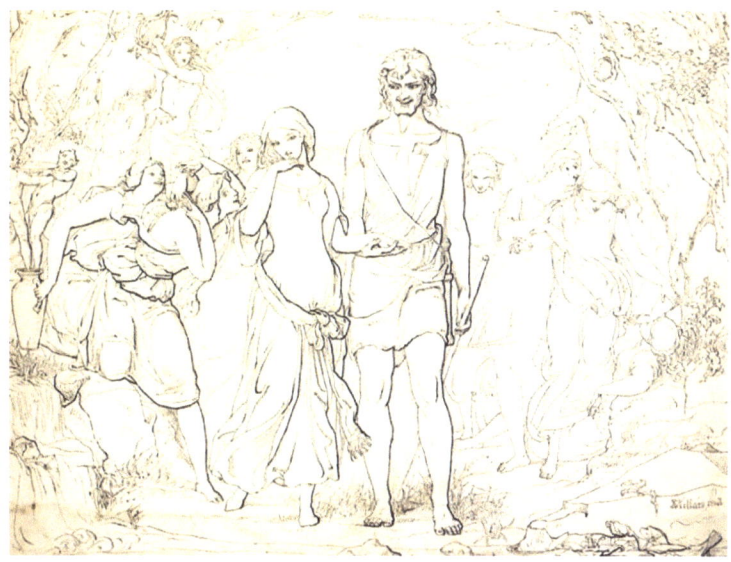

Cymon And Iphigenia, Study--1847--Romanticism--sketch and study

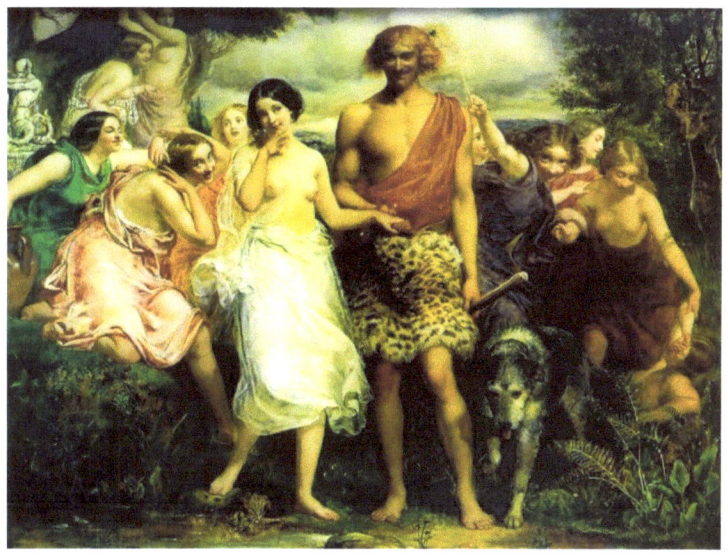

Cymon And Iphigenia--1848-1851-- Romanticism

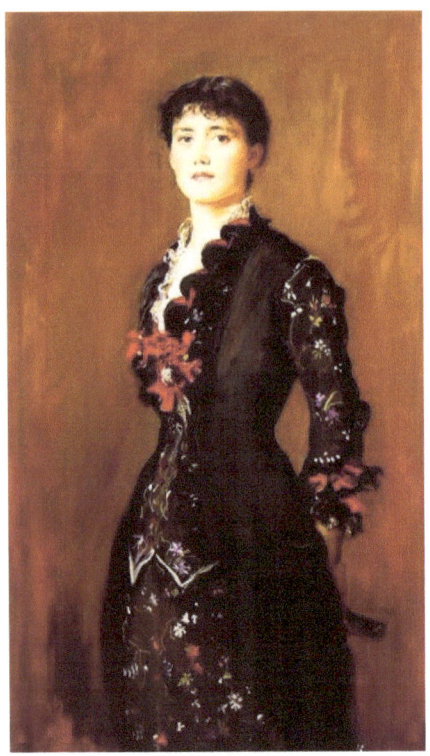

Louise Jopling-- Romanticism

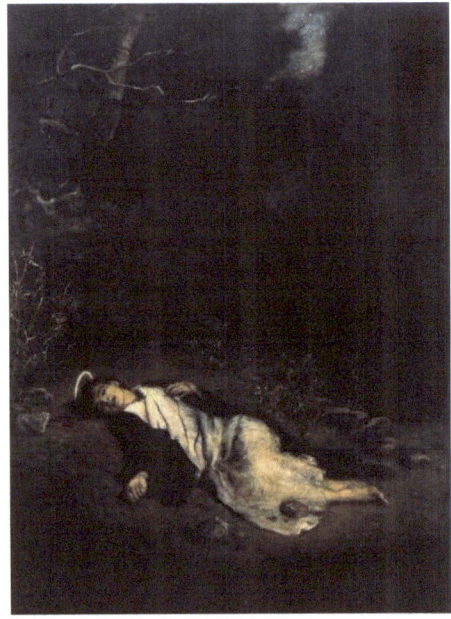

Saint Stephen--1895

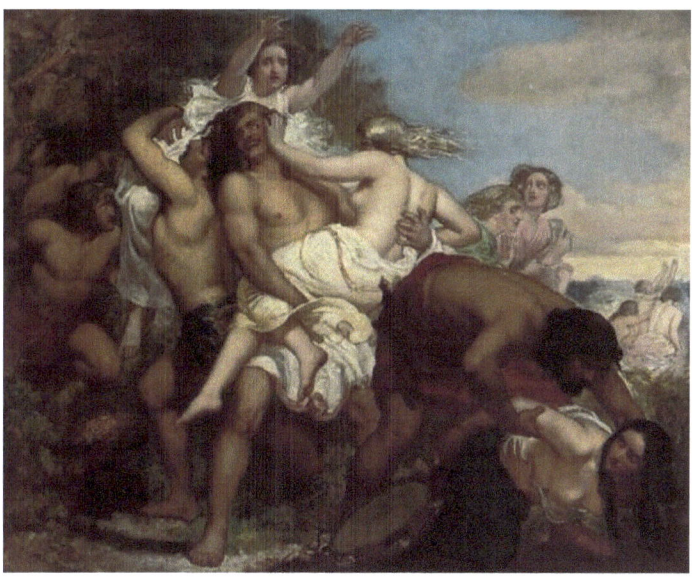

The Tribe Of Benjamin Seizing The Daughter Of Shiloh--1847--

Romanticism

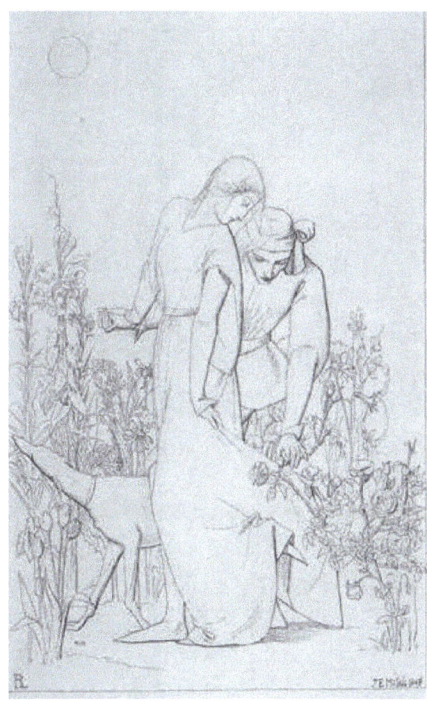

My Beautiful Lady--1848--Romanticism-- sketch and study

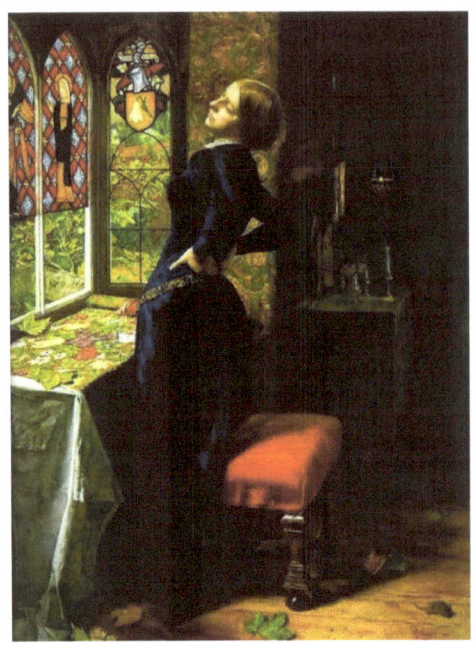

Mariana In The Moated Grange--1851--Romanticism

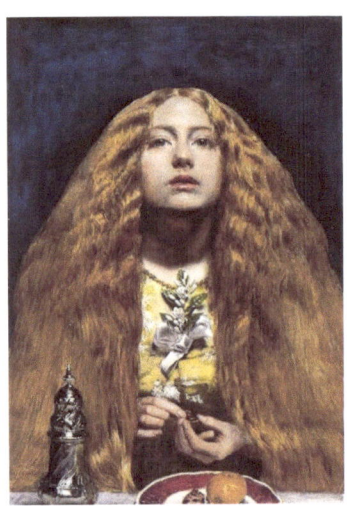

The Bridesmaid--1851-- Romanticism

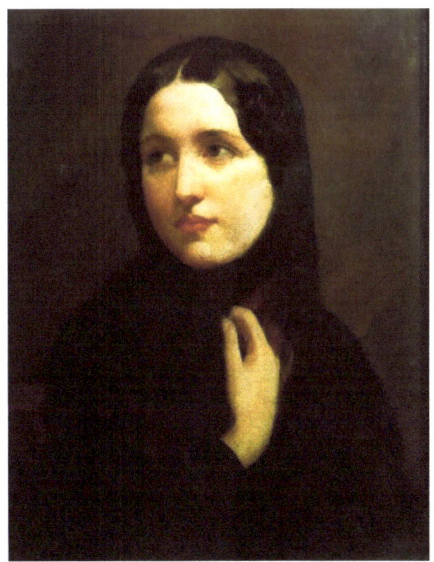

Mariana--1851--Realism

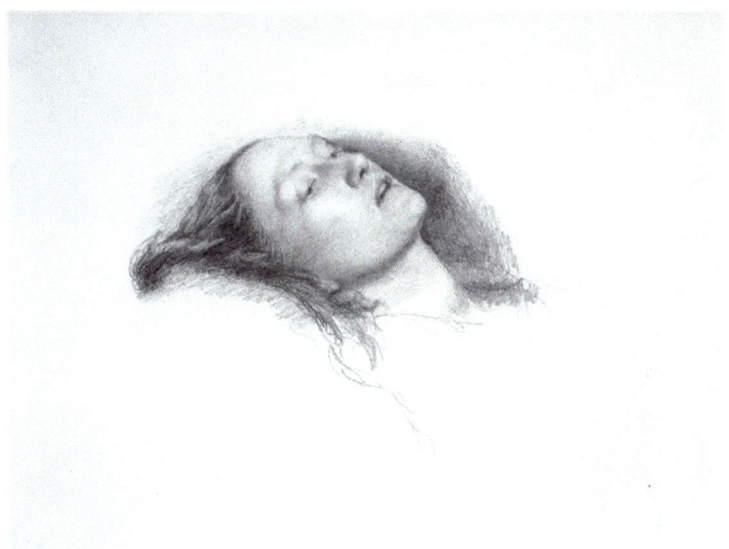

Study For Ophelia--1852-- Romanticism

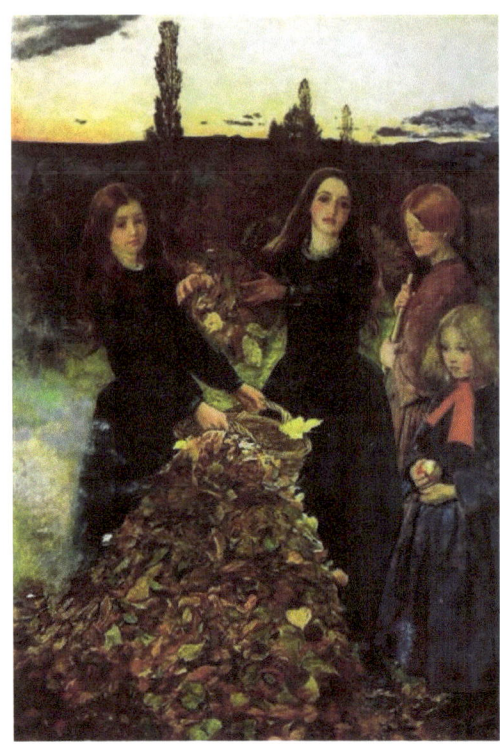

Autumn Leaves-- 1855-1856--Romanticism

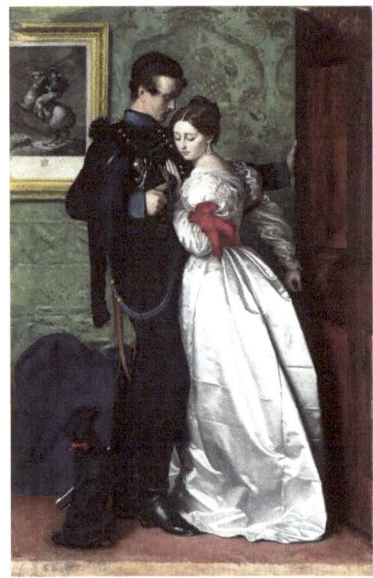

The Black Brunswicker--1860--Romanticism

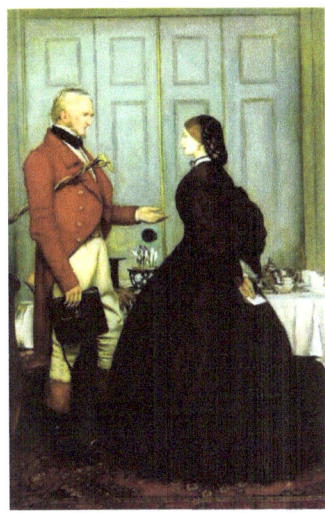

Trust Me--1862--Romanticism

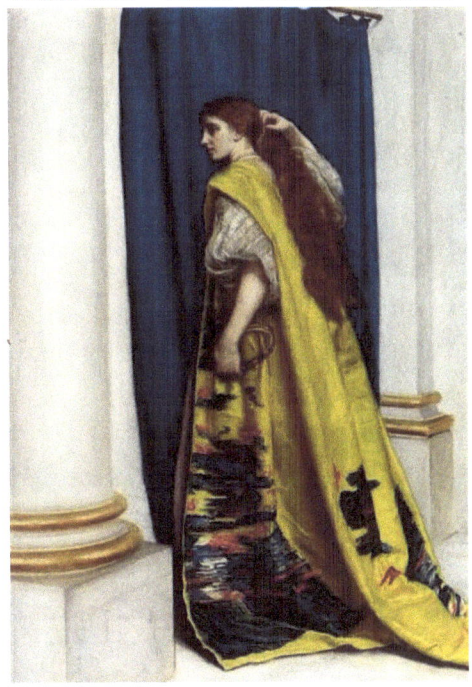

Esther-- Romanticism

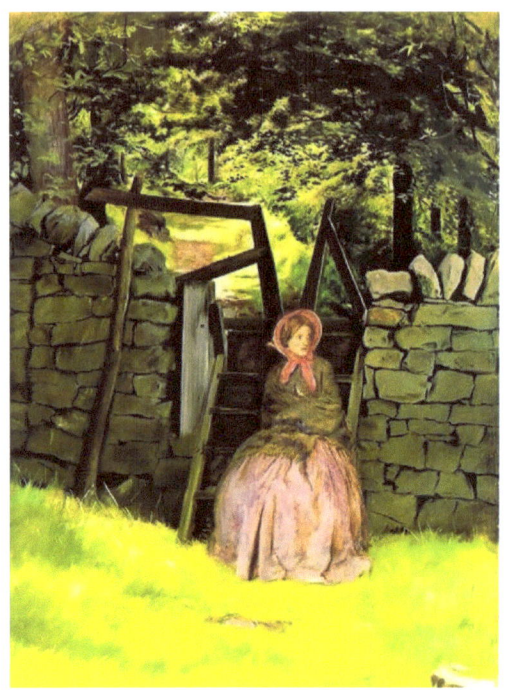

Waiting--1854--Romanticism

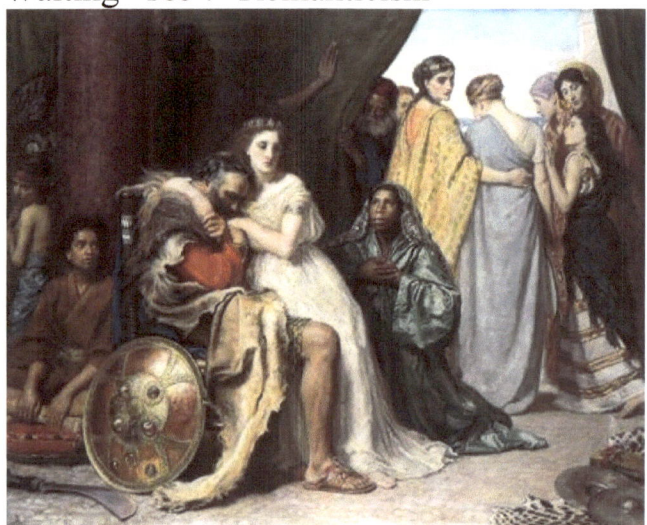

Jephthah--1867-- Romanticism

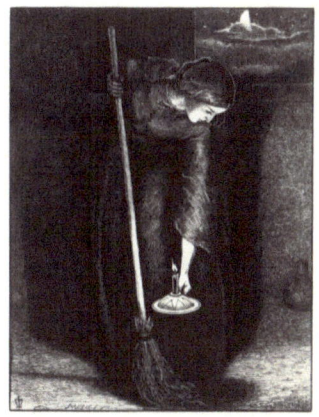

The Lost Piece Of Silver--1864--Romanticism

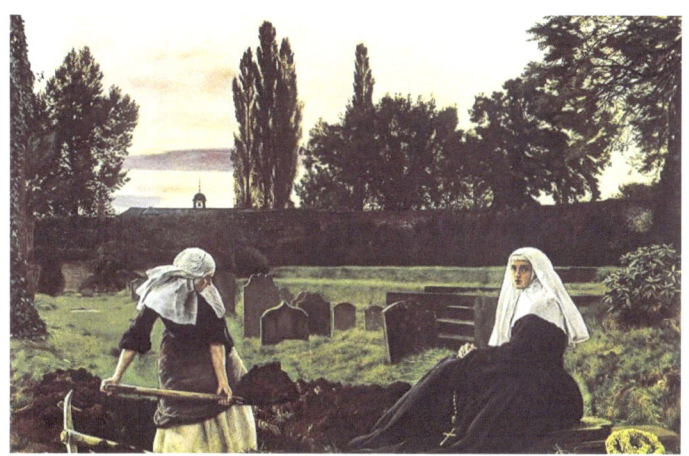

The Vale Of Rest--1858-1859-- Realism

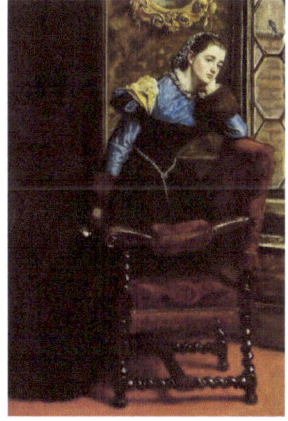

Swallow, Swallow--1864--Romanticism

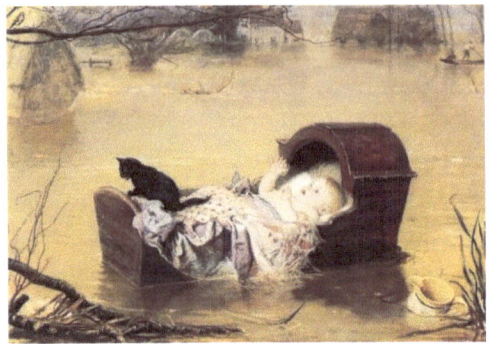

A Flood-- 1870-- Romanticism

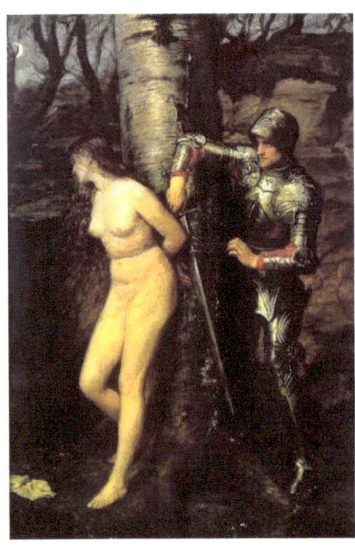

The Knight Errant--1870--Romanticism

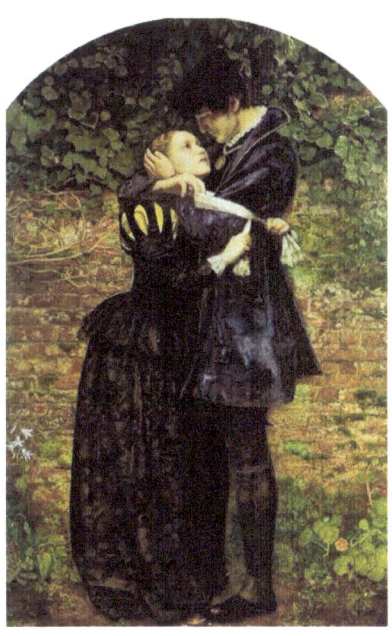

A Huguenot, On St. Bartholomew's Day, Refusing To Shield Himself From Danger By Wearing The Roman Catholic Badge

1852--Romanticism

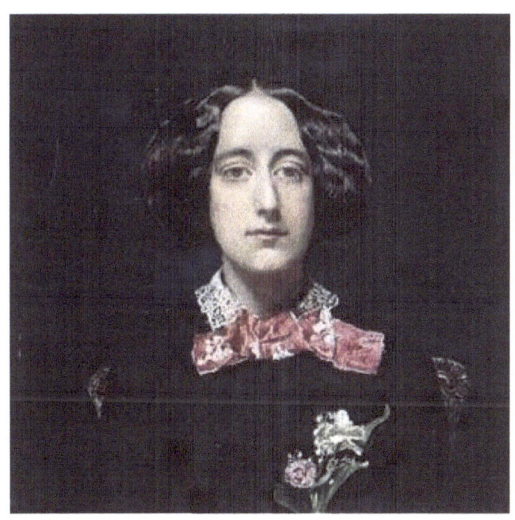

Emily Patmore--1851-- Realism

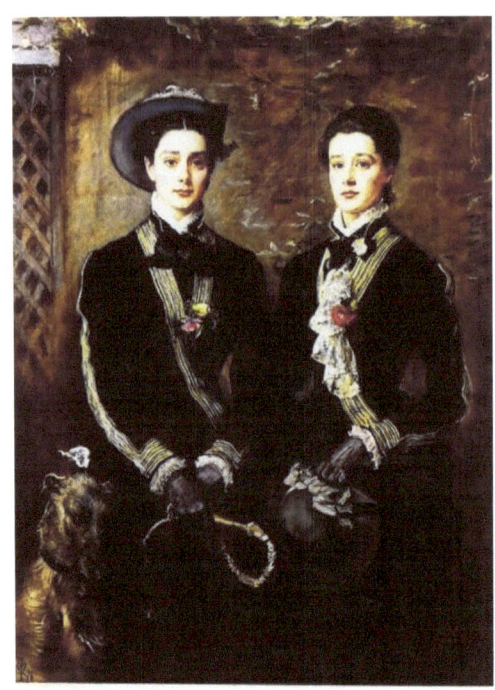

Twins (Grace And Kate Hoare)-- 1876-- Realism

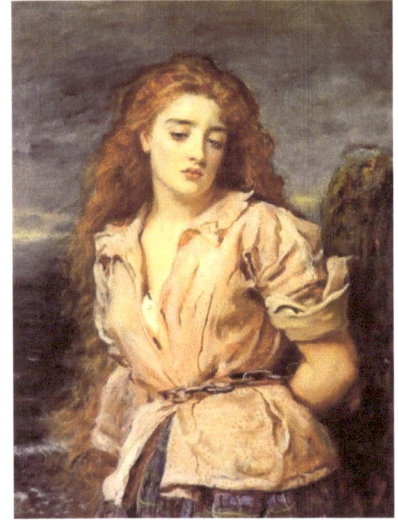

The Matyr Of The Solway-- 1871--Romanticism

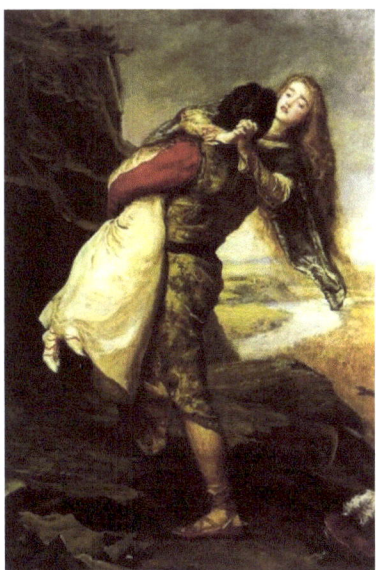

The Crown Of Love--1875--Romanticism

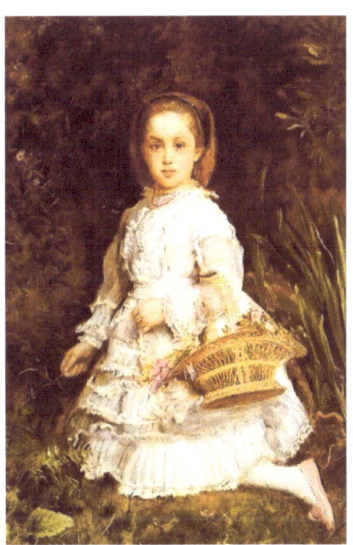

Portrait Of Gracia Lees--1875-- Realism

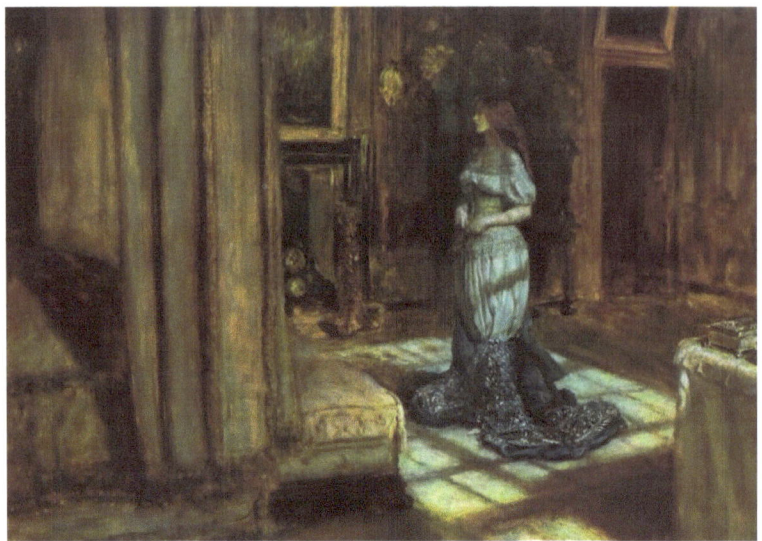

The Eve Of Saint Agnes--1863-- Realism

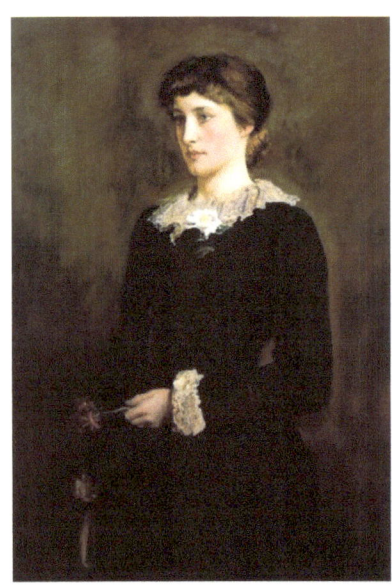

A Jersey Lily, Portrait Of Lillie Langtry--1878-- Realism

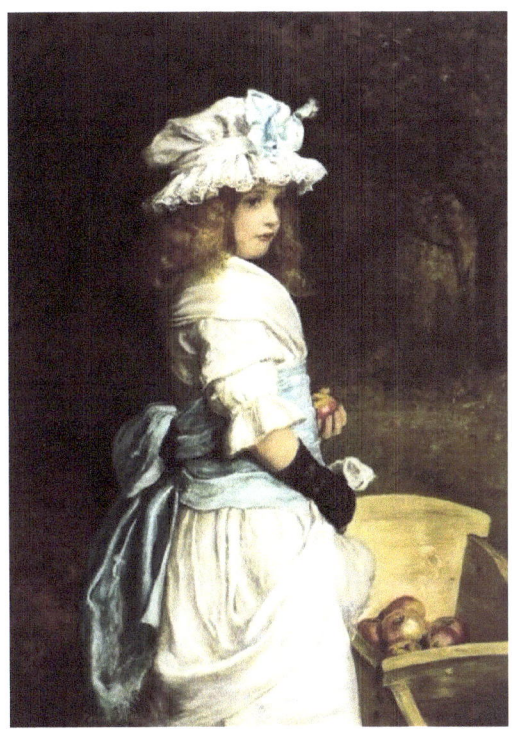

Pomona--1882--Style: Realism

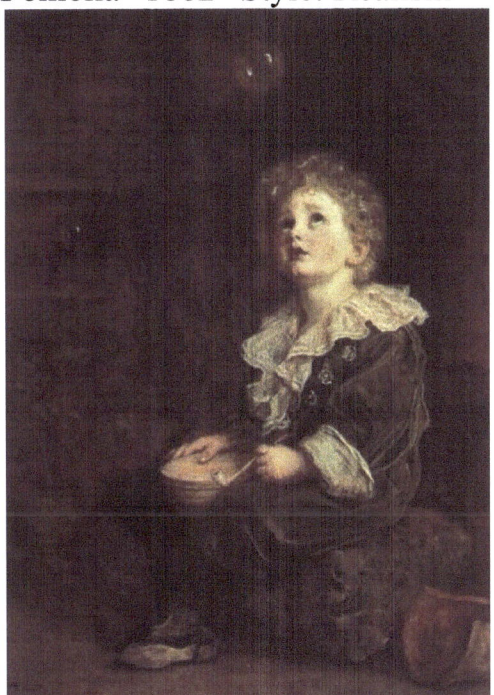

Bubbles--1886-- Realism

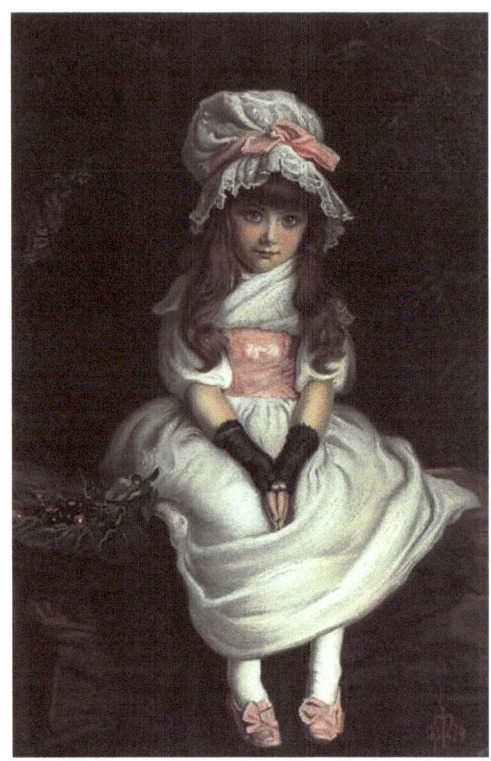

Cherry Ripe-- 1879-- Realism

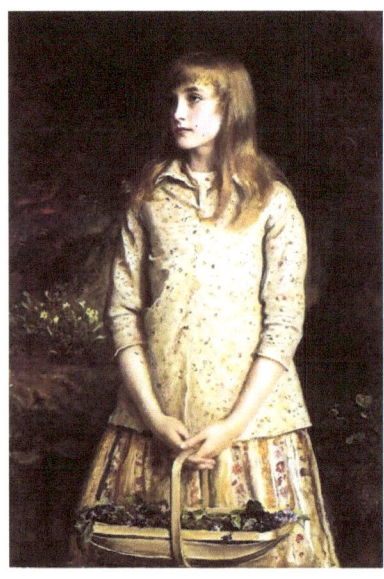

Sweetest Eyes That Were Ever Seen…--1881--Realism

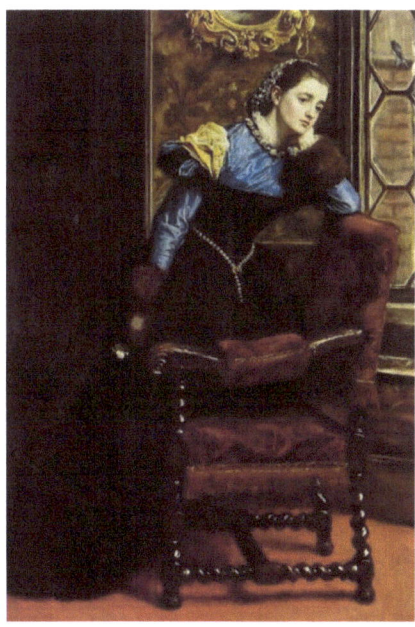

Swallow, Swallow--1864--Romanticism

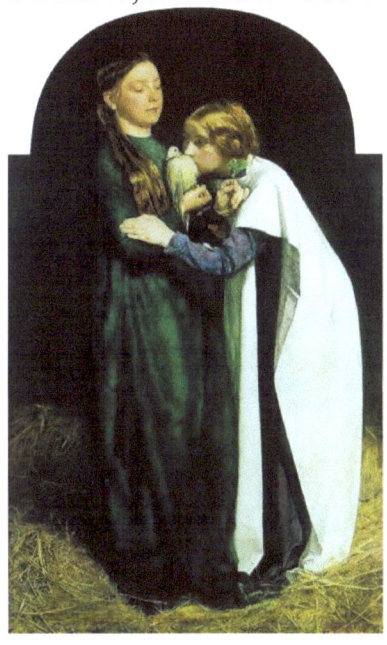

The Return Of The Dove To The Ark--1851--Romanticism

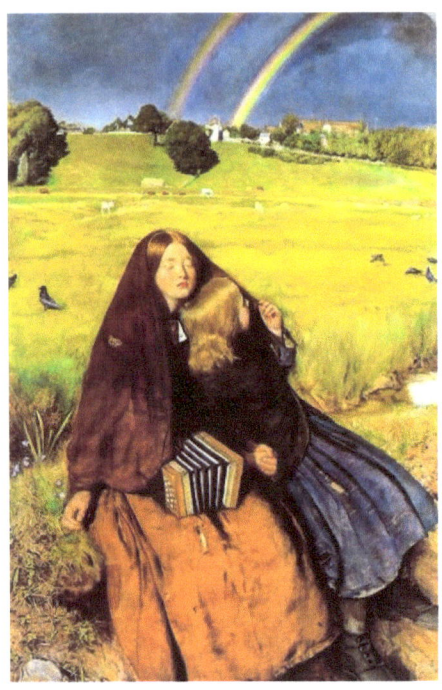

The Blind Girl--1854-1856--Romanticism

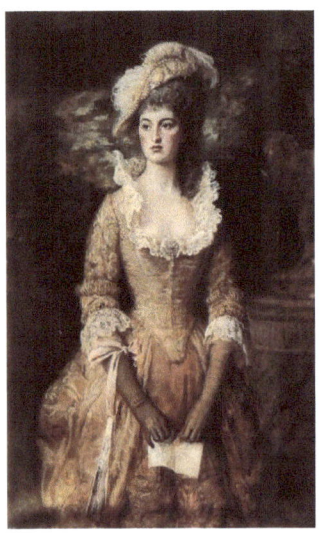

Clarissa--1887--Romanticism

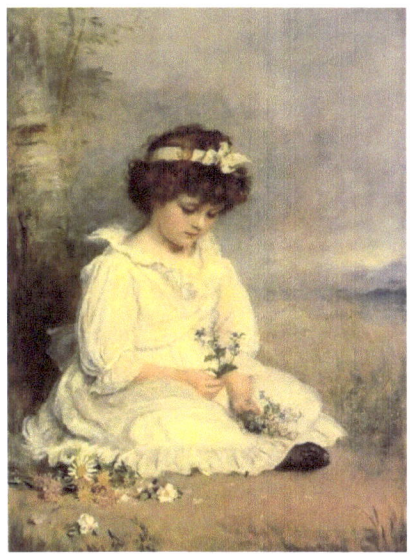

Little Speedwell's Darling Blue--1892-- Realism

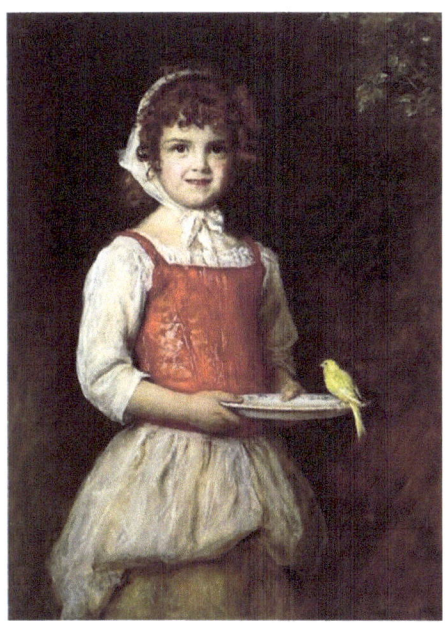

Merry--1893-- Realism

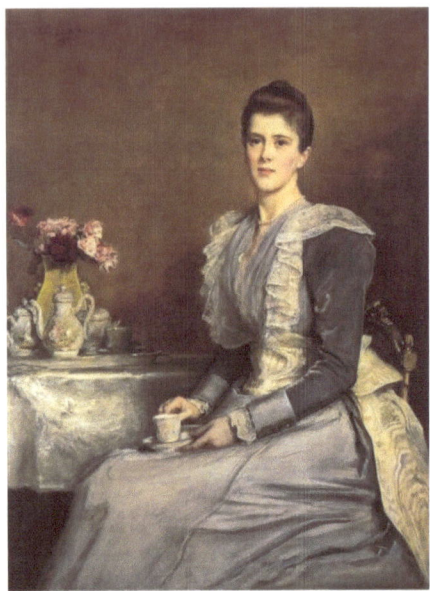

Mary Chamberlain--1891-- Realism

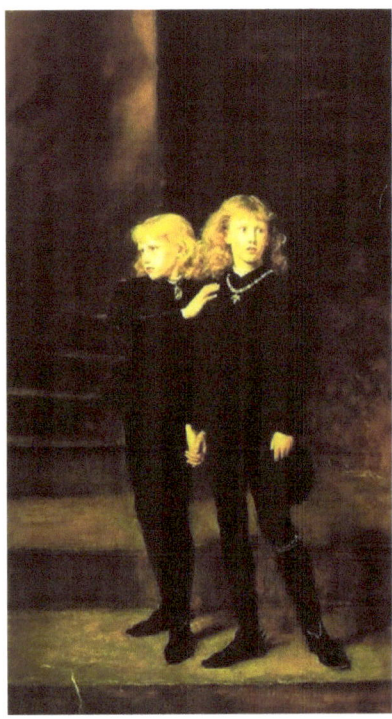

Princes In The Tower--Romanticism

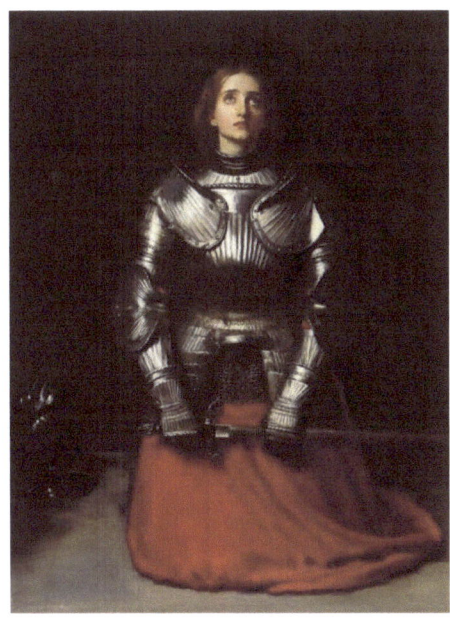

Joan Of Arc--Romanticism

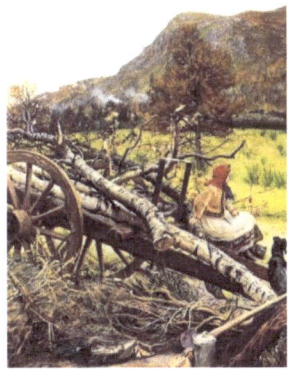

Winter Fuel--1873-- Realism

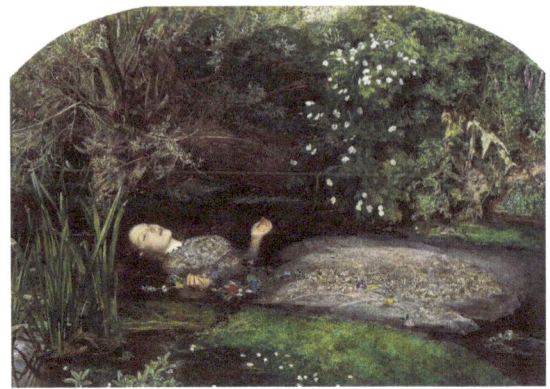

Ophelia--1852-- Romanticism

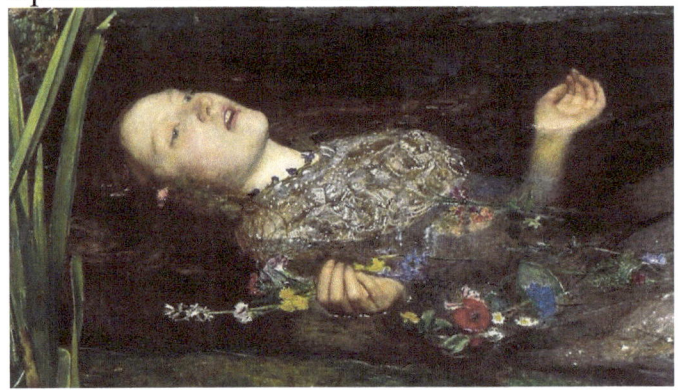

Ophelia (detail)-- 1851-52

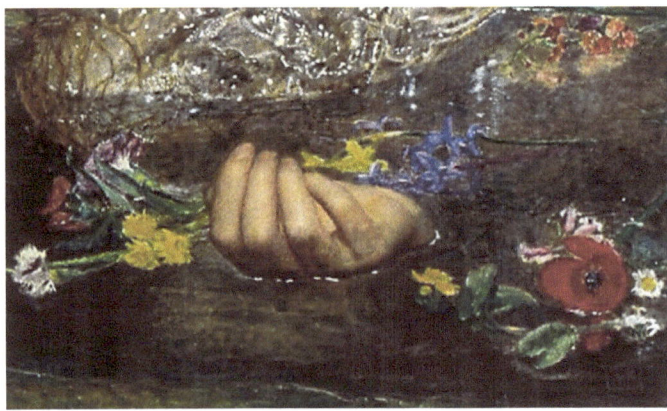

Ophelia (detail)--1851-52

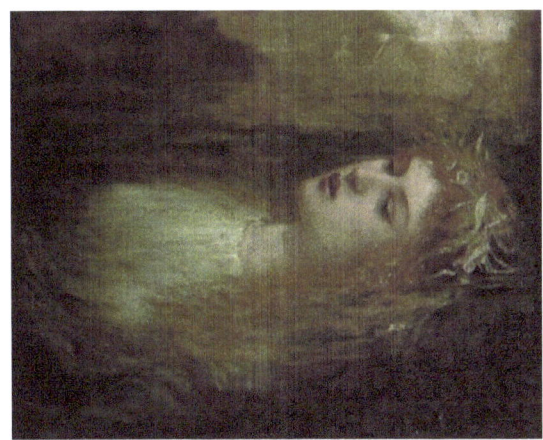

Ophelia, 1872–1872

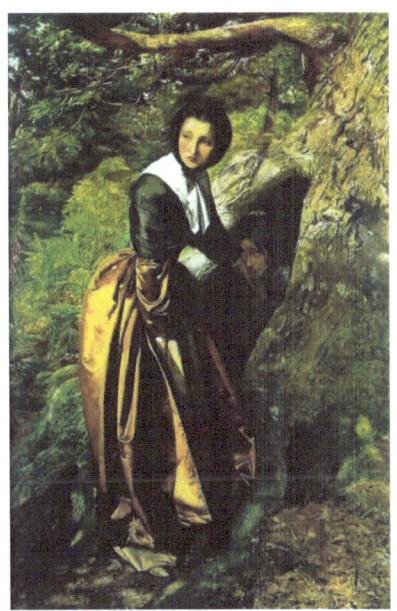

The Royalist-- Romanticism

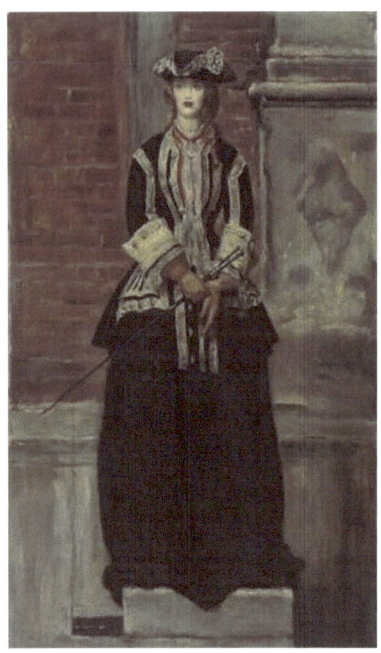

Charlie is my Darling

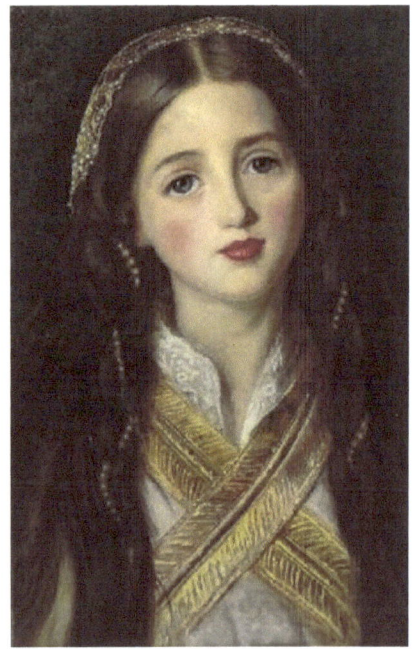

Alice Gray

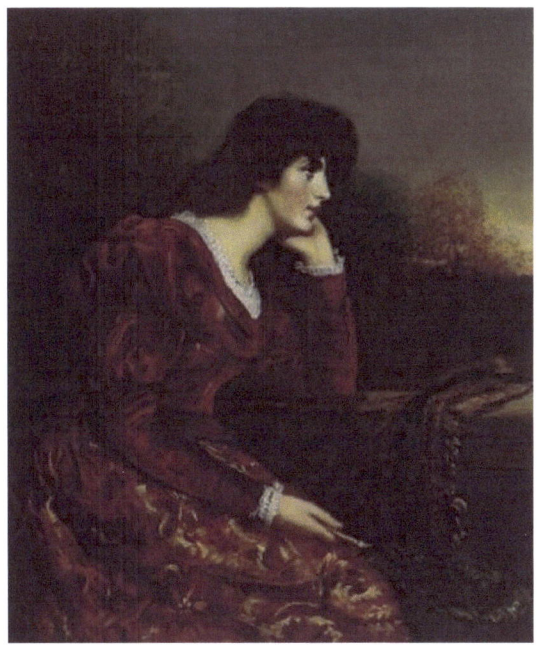

Forlorn, or I am never merry when I hear sweet music-1888

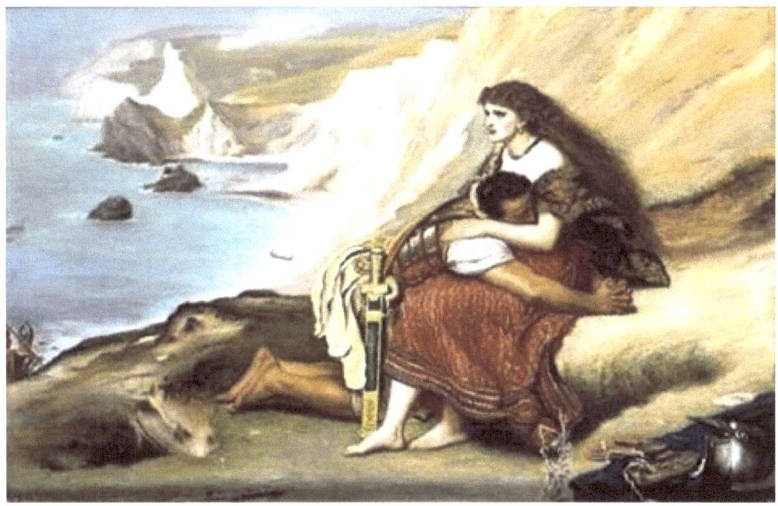

The Romans leaving Britain

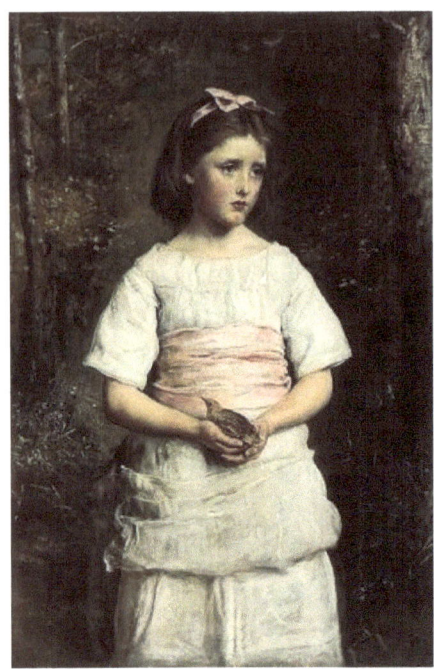

Dropped from the nest--1883

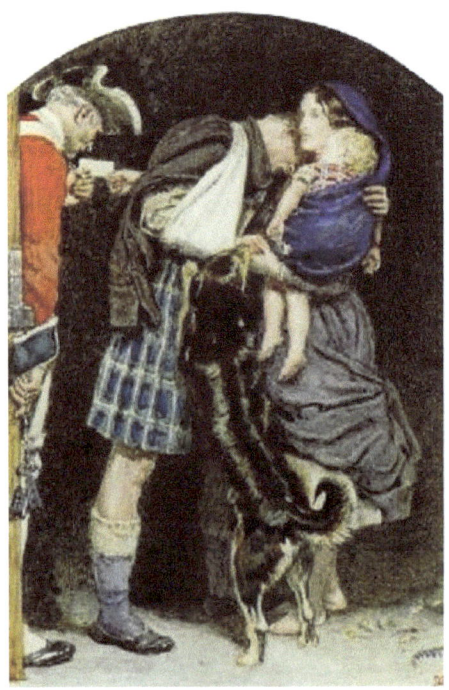

The order of release

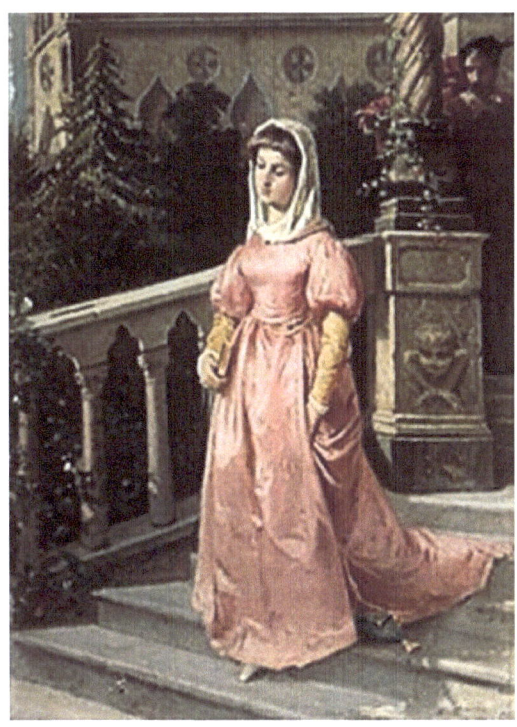

Ung dam i Venedig

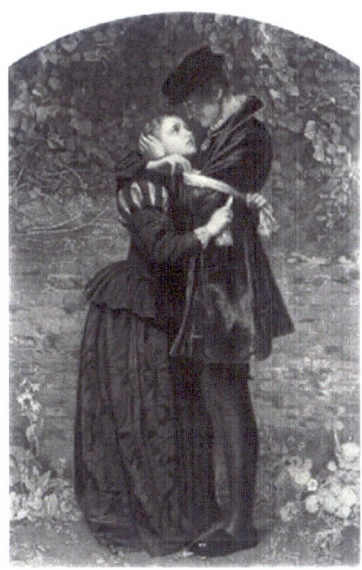

The Huguenot, by Thomas Oldham Barlow, 1857

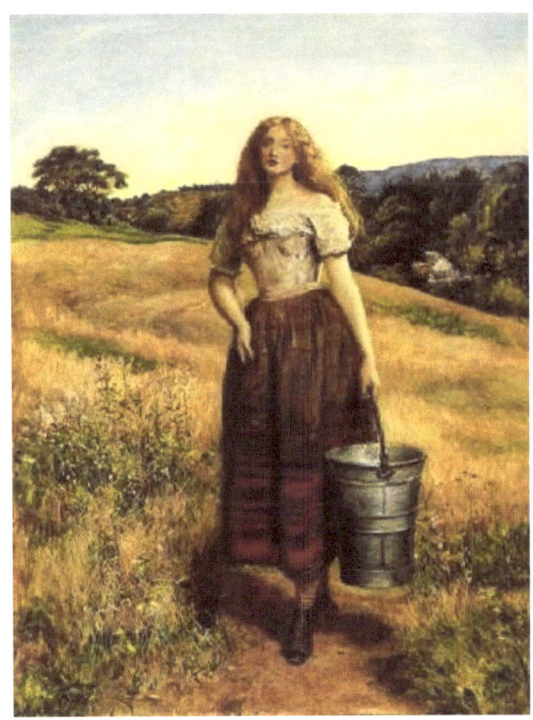

The farmer's daughter

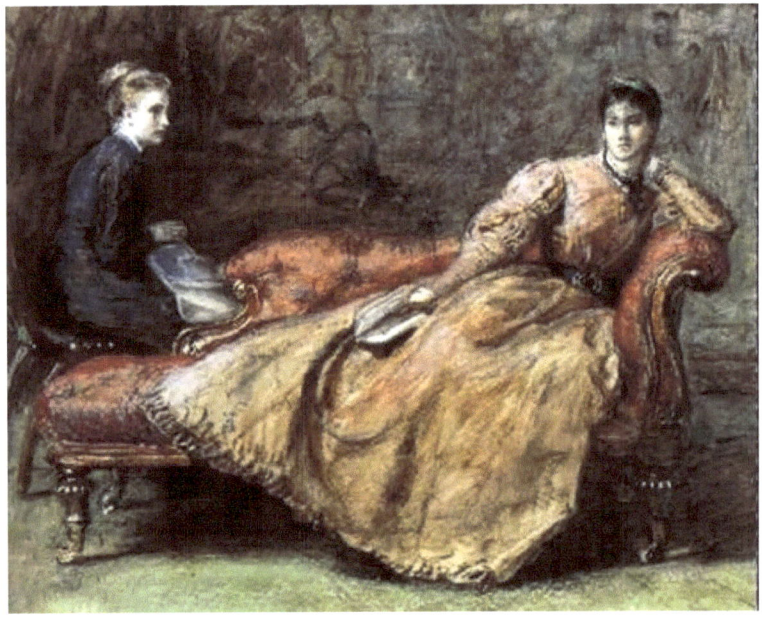

The end of the chapter, 1869

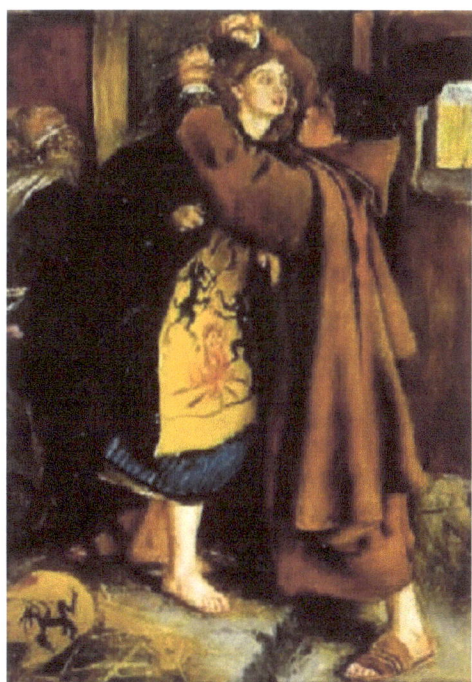

The escape of a heretic

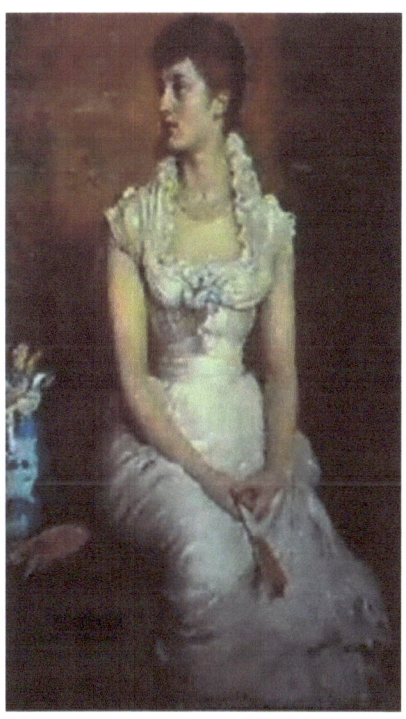

lady Campbell (Nina Lehmann)--1884

www.ingramcontent.com/pod-product-compliance
Lightning Source LLC
Chambersburg PA
CBHW050413180526

45159CB00005B/2255